The Instant Wine Connoisseur

*A Practical Guide to Tasting,
Buying and Cooking With Wine*

The Instant Wine Connoisseur

A Practical Guide to Tasting,
Buying and Cooking With Wine

Mervyn L. Hecht

BookWorld Press, Inc.
Sarasota, Florida

Published by BookWorld Press, Inc.
1933 Whitfield Park Loop • Sarasota, Florida 34243
Orders 800/444-2524 • Order Fax 800/777-2525
International 941/758-8094 • International Fax 941/753-9396

ISBN 1-884962-08-4
Library of Congress Catalog Number 96-094610
Cover design by Pearl & Associates, Inc.
Manufactured in the United States of America

Hecht, Mervyn
The Instant Wine Connoisseur:
A Practical Guide to Tasting, Buying and Cooking With Wine
Mervyn Hecht
p. cm.
ISBN 1-884962-08-4

1. Wine and wine making. 2. Cookery—Wine. I. Title

TP548.H43 1997   641.2'2
QBI96-40242

Mervyn L. Hecht is the wine buyer for a California wine import company. Although based in Santa Monica, California, he and his wife live and work in France several months each year. He is the author of a number of books and articles on various subjects.

Contents

Introduction

Questions You Should Ask

This is a book about the tastes of wines. The object of the book is to help you, the wine drinker, identify and remember the most important wines, so that wine labels and wine lists begin to make some sense. But I'm trying to not write a book that requires you to have to study and memorize in order to understand and remember wines. Because people don't do that, most wine drinkers are lost when reading a wine list or looking at a wine label. So what I do in this book is explain about taste and how to do it, then lead you into tasting the differences among the major wines. By focusing only on the most important wines and how they taste, I hope to avoid cluttering up your mind with more information than you need. In other words, I hope to impart a methodology, and just enough information for you to get started so that you can enjoy the great pleasures of wine.

In addition, I discuss in the book what I think are the most important aspects of wine customs, such as which wines to drink with which foods, which wines to decant, and which wines to age. Finally, I briefly discuss general health concerns about drinking wine—in fact, is it good for us as well as delightful?

To accomplish these goals I believe that the prospective wine drinker will need to have a few questions answered, such as the following:

Question One:

Why Another Book About Wines?

Every month I get a book by mail that is nothing more than a long list of wine books. There must be hundreds listed, and there are many books in print that are not listed. Just this month I myself bought three books about wine, and what wonderful works they are! But two of them are really big, and are going to take a long time for me to read. I'll enjoy every minute of it.

One of these two books reads more like a novel; it's a history of the Zinfandel grape in

California. By the time I'm done reading this book I'll probably know more about the history of Zinfandel than I do about my own family's history.

As interesting as these books are, none of them focuses on the practical problems that most wine drinkers face, such as:

- How do the wines on a restaurant wine list (or in a store) taste, and how can I remember the tastes?
- When ordering wine in a restaurant, which wine should I order, and what factors should I take into consideration?
- Which wines match well with which foods?
- What are reasonable prices for various wines?
- What should I know about storing and serving wine?
- Is wine good for you—or is it harmful?

These are the issues that most wine drinkers face. So while production methods and Chateau history make for interesting reading, as a practical matter they don't help us to be able to look at a wine list in a restaurant and imagine the taste of the wines listed so that we can decide which one to order. Certainly that's what we do with the food on the menu: we think about the taste of salmon, or beef, and choose one or the other. You probably can remember what salmon tasted like the last time you ate it. Remembering the taste of wine is much more difficult for most people, and as a result they order wine based on color (red or white) and price.

It is not clear why there is such a difference between ordering off the food menu, and ordering off the wine list. It's not that there are more wines than foods. I read somewhere that there are dozens of types of shrimp, and I know there are lots of varieties of apples. But when I see a shrimp dish listed on the menu, or an apple dessert, I have some idea what it is going to taste like. That's because there is an apple taste and a shrimp taste, and I remember them. And like most people, even though there is a difference in taste between apples, I generally remember which ones are more crisp and tart, and which more soft and sweet.

The problem for the wine drinker is, I believe, that the label on the bottle doesn't say anything that is the equivalent of "apple" or "shrimp." While some great connoisseurs may be able to identify a particular "Chateau Margaux taste," I can only tell that it's probably a Bordeaux. And even then I might be wrong, and it might turn out to be a California Cabernet Sauvignon that's been blended in the Bordeaux manner. But because both of those wines are made primarily from the Cabernet Sauvignon grape, they have similar tastes.

Since particular grapes do have a distinctive taste, if you know what grape or blend of grapes a wine is made from, it helps to anticipate what it will taste like.

Yes, there are differences between vineyards, producers, years, and geography. But there is a "Cabernet Sauvignon taste," and generally I can tell it when I taste it. In other words, to focus the mind on the taste of a wine, I need to know the taste of the primary grape from which the wine is made. For example, it's difficult to distinguish a Barolo from a Barbaresco, because both are made from the same grape, but it's not hard to tell either of those wines from a Chianti, which is made from a different grape.

So I decided to write a book that describes, in SIMPLE terms, the tastes of the primary wine grapes, and the wines we see most often on wine lists and in wine stores. And I decided NOT to include a lot of information about the climate, the soil, the manufacturing processes, and all the other information that makes other peoples' books such interesting reading. Instead, I include just a few interesting facts about only the most important grapes—just enough so that something about each important grape stays in the mind.

Nor do I attempt in this book to discuss every grape from which wines are made—or even most of them. There are dozens, (hundreds?), of wine grapes, and that is one reason why it is difficult to buy wine or order it off a wine list: there are too many, with too many confusing names. My goal in this book is to select the most important grapes —those from which the most important wines are made that we customarily drink with food. My hope is that armed with this information, you will be able to find a few wines on each wine list with familiar names that you can associate with a particular taste.

Only then does it make sense to move on to evaluate the year, the producer, and the price, from which a more discriminating decision can be made when buying a bottle or ordering wine with dinner. In other words, if you can mentally taste the wine, you can tell how much you are going to like it, and mentally pair it with the food you plan to eat. Then you can evaluate the price, to see if it is reasonable, in light of the reputation of the producer and the vintage.

In addition to the problem of connecting the visual sense (reading the list or label) to an anticipated taste, there are a lot of social conventions, "snobbery," and folklore about wine that makes many drinkers wary of doing something gauche. Does veal require red or white wine? Should Port be served before or after dinner? Should a 1982 Chateauneuf-du-Pape be decanted or served from the bottle?

These are the types of practical questions I hope to answer in this book.

Question Two:

What Do I Need to Know to Buy A Bottle of Wine Intelligently?

The first thing you should want to know is "What is it going to taste like?" In order to get to that point I discovered that you have to understand a little bit about the physiology of tasting: how the tongue, eye, nose brain AND MIND work together to create a "taste." As I explain more completely below, some of what we taste is from the tastebuds on the tongue, most is from sensors in the nose, and a bit is added by the mind from what we see, and what we know from current information and prior experience.

Secondly, you might want to know what special conventions are generally recommended to enjoy wine, and which wines traditionally go with what foods. A few recipes that use wine for flavor will help in this connection.

Finally, more and more wine drinkers are asking health related questions about wine. For example, one common question is "should I drink wine if I'm taking antibiotics?" There are a number of medical conditions, such as diabetes and liver conditions, that raise questions about the good sense of drinking wine. My wife keeps telling me that I drink too much, my friend the pathologist tells me that autopsies on drunks reveal extraordinarily clear arteries, and I read in my newspaper that French people who drink red wine have less heart disease, in spite of a high cholesterol diet. What is the latest medical information on drinking wine, and how should we apply it to our lives?

Question Three:

Why All This Fuss About Wine Anyway?

For me, that's the most interesting question of all. Grapes are the number one agricultural crop in California. About 100 BILLION dollars worth of grapes are sold on the wholesale market worldwide each year. People have been drinking wine for more than 5,000 years. Noah planted a vineyard 4,000 years ago, produced some wine and got drunk from it. More time, money, and land are devoted to wine than to either sex or religion! WHY? I have a few ideas, and I'll share them with you in the following pages.

—*Port Grimaud, France, Jan. 1996*

Taste

Section One:

The How

Taste is a subjective experience. For this reason we can never be sure it's the same for me as it is for you. In fact, we can be sure that some tastes will give me more pleasure than they will for you, and vice versa. But because of our common taste experiences and common language we can communicate the similarities and differences, and thereby increase our understanding. To have the common experiences, however, requires that each of us have some memory bank of tastes to draw against. As a result of common experiences and communication, objective standards begin to mold the subjectivity of individual views. In other words, interaction with other people has an effect on our reaction to the subjective taste of wine, and can give it more meaning and enjoyment.

Let me give you an example. Years ago certain producers in Greece stored their wines in barrels made from wood that gave the wine the taste of the resin in the wood. For many people the flavor of resin, which is a bit like turpentine, is very off-putting in a wine. But lots of Greek wine drinkers in that region got used to the flavor, and began to look forward to it. Over time, other people began to associate that flavor in wine with certain Greek foods. Today if a French wine tasted of resin it would be sent back. But retsina from Greece is sold all over the world, and many of us enjoy it with Greek food. The common experience of drinking wine with that particular flavor, eventually dissemi- nated to others, created a new objective stan- dard, or expectation in our memory bank, for the taste of resin with Greek food.

Because taste is experiential, it is best if these "common experiences" arise by actually tasting the wine. No matter how many books we read, we can't learn to ride a bicycle or hit a golf drive well until we do it a few times. Even if I tell you that the taste of resin in wine goes well with Greek food, you're not going to like it unless you drink it a few times with Greek food—any more than you liked spinach the first time your mother told you it was good for you, or the first time a Japanese friend offered me some sea urchin sushi!

In fact, to create such a memory bank requires not only that we have the experience, but that we focus our attention on it in special ways. If each of us walks past a shoe store every day for a year, but we don't notice it, the experience will not create a useful memory. Focus—or attention—is the first step.

For this reason, when tasting wine, certain rituals have become customary. If you follow them your attention will be focused on the elements of taste, and those elements will begin to stick in your mind.

A typical list of rules to follow to taste, evaluate, and commit tastes to memory is as follows:

1. Clear your palate and taste buds with a glass of water. Pour some wine into a bowl shaped glass, but fill the glass only one-third full, to leave enough room in the glass for the aroma of the wine to gather. The wine should be slightly cooler than room temperature. Some people like white wine as cool as 50 degrees.

2. **LOOK** at the wine, preferably with a white background, and make a mental note of the color. Note both the color at the center, and the color at the edges. Older red wine tends to turn orange or brown at the edges. Certain white wines tend to pale at the edges. In addition to the color, note the clarity (or dullness or cloudiness) of the wine, to make sure it is well made and not spoiled. Finally, look at the viscosity, or body (from a visual point of view) to

anticipate the feel of the liquid on the tongue.

3. **SMELL** the wine, and verbalize your reaction. Verbalizing makes it easier to remember. Since our vocabulary doesn't really contain precise words for the odors of wine, it is necessary to use words that are analogous to the odors of the wine, such as floral, fruity, chocolate, earthy, etc. No wine tastes like chocolate, but there are flavors in some wines that are reminiscent of chocolate. The smell of wine is referred to professionally as its "NOSE," or "bouquet." Experts separate the various smells into two categories, one based on the smell of the grape, and the other based on the aging characteristics of the wine, such as oak, or the special bouquet derived from long aging in the bottle.

4. **SWIRL** the wine and smell it again, since aeration sometimes affects the nose of the wine.

5. **SIP** some of the wine into the mouth with air, then let it run over the tongue. Pay attention to the first tastes. The chemical contact of the wine on the various tongue sensors (sweet, sour, salty and bitter) combines with the nose to create a first taste. It used to be thought that only these four primary tastes came from the tongue. Recent scientific studies conducted on the taste buds of eels (which apparently have very large taste buds, and are easier to study) have shown that the combinations of tastes in the mouth create a much greater variety of tastes than originally thought possible. This first taste of wine is sometimes referred to by professionals as its "entry."

6. Swirl the wine in the mouth, then **SWALLOW** it. Note the change in taste from the first taste, and pay attention to the differences in the aftertaste, and the duration and strength of the aftertaste. Wine with more intense fruit and adequate acidity will have a stron-

ger and longer aftertaste, enhancing the pleasure of the wine. The taste the wine leaves in the mouth after swallowing it (or spitting it out, in a professional tasting) is what we refer to as the "aftertaste." The aftertaste is very important in tasting wines, food and drink in general.

7. Think and **TALK** about the taste, paying attention to at least the following six elements:

(a) How intense is the flavor.

(b) Is the wine sweet, medium, or dry; ("dry" refers to a lack of sweetness).

(c) How tart is the wine. Tartness is caused by acidity, and is very prized in some wines. Think of orange juice, and how good the tart taste is with the fruit flavor.

(d) How astringent is the wine; astringency is usually found in red wines known for long life, and is a result of tannin from grape skins. Young full bodied wines are often more tannic in the first few years. After a time, the tannins soften. Coffee and tea have a tannic taste that many people like.

(e) Is the wine balanced? The most pleasing wines have a balance between the elements described above. The proportions, however, are a subjective matter, and preferences vary widely among wine lovers.

(f) finally, what is the impression of the aftertaste, the taste that remains after swallowing? A pleasant lingering flavor is one of the pleasures of fine wines.

So far we've been talking about the taste of wine. But all of this applies to food and drink in general. One of the benefits of learning to appreciate the taste of wine is that it enhances our appreciation of foods and beverages. For example, try the procedure above with orange juice. When I did it recently I discovered that the orange juice had a fruity, sweet nose, but with less orange to it than I had expected. The first taste was of orange, but the aftertaste was long and tart, with a flavor I connect more with pineapple than with orange. I was surprised at the acidity on the tongue, and how reminiscent it was of the aftertaste of a white wine that is high in acid. On another occasion I noticed how much sweeter this orange juice was than the last one I had drunk.

If you begin to focus your attention on taste, you will be surprised how quickly you can begin to identify the major spices in foods, such as onion, thyme, cinnamon, basil, tarragon, etc. And practicing on foods is good practice for wine. The fact is that an appreciation of taste in general makes dining more pleasurable, and helps us to eat more slowly and to eat less, without any reduction of pleasure.

Section Two:

The Why

My mother used to say that it's easier to follow rules if you understand the reasons behind them. So why do we look at the color, swirl the wine in the glass, smell first, and talk afterward?

Taste is a very complex activity involving sight, sound, texture, taste buds, mouth sensors, memory, and—above all—smell. Let's briefly examine each of these elements:

1. For wine tasting, sound is the least important part. Some people don't like crunchy foods, and soft versus hard can be determined partly by sound. Since all wine is liquid the sound doesn't vary enough to be a factor.

2. Texture is part of what the mouth sensors sense. The thickness of a liquid, called viscosity, plays a small part in wine tasting. Some wines are sensed as thicker, or

more viscous, than others. This is associated with the "body" of the wine, although not necessarily with the strength of the flavor. Wines with more viscosity, or body, are usually perceived as being "richer" tasting, because more viscosity is usually associated with more extract, and thus stronger flavor.

Viscosity is usually tested by wine drinkers by swirling the wine in the glass, and then looking at the "legs," the wine that runs down the inside of the glass after swirling. The existence of "legs" is an indication of a viscous wine, a wine that will be expected to have a full bodied texture.

Viscosity plays a minor part in wine tasting. The small part it does play is confounded or reinforced by what we see. Wines from southern, hotter regions tend toward more viscosity, while wines from the northern, cooler climates tend toward "thinness."

3. Sight is often a major confound in taste. Some kids won't eat spinach because of its looks, not because of its taste. Dark brown foods are often considered unappetizing, as are meats dripping blood. Without looking first, some people can't tell a red wine from a white wine. People used to drinking mild rosé are often surprised when they taste a strong flavored rosé.

Where sight is helpful in tasting is in aiding memory. The visual analysis of the color and viscosity of the wine brings forth memories of similar wines from the past, and prepares the mouth and the taste buds for the pleasure to come, much as Pavlov's bell prepared his dogs' taste buds for dinner. Appreciation of color and associations from memory are part of the pleasure of wine.

4. By and large, it's the combination of tongue sensors and smell that creates the unique taste of wine. Of these, the smell sensors are somewhat more important, and

these are among the least understood of our senses. When we
swallow a liquid, some of the
molecules of the liquid are forced
up into the nasal passages, where
they trigger a signal directly to
the limbic system in the brain, the
seat of emotions, sexuality,
memory and drive.

While not well understood from a
physiological point of view, some
of the primitive significance of
smell is well known. From an
evolutionary point of view smell
has great significance. It is the
oldest sense and has the most
direct access to the brain of any of
our senses. Certainly smell was
involved in sexual selection and in
the testing of food and drink
before eating or drinking. Even
now perfume manufacturers would
have us believe that the right
smell will create sexual interest in
others. And my wife insists on
smelling any suspect food before
eating it, "just to be sure it's safe."

Don't underestimate the power of
our noses. I read somewhere that
sharks can smell blood when there
is one part in several million in
water. That's only slightly better
than some wine tasters who, after
a taste, can tell the year and maker
of the wine. Through smell a baby
finds its mother's breast, and a
mother can identify her baby in
the dark. In fact, one percent of all
our genes is devoted to detecting
odors, and this is the largest gene
family we know of in mammals.
According to nature, smell is our
most important method of contact
with the outside world![2]

But because sight and touch have
become more important in today's
world (certainly in sexual selection) we've neglected the power of
our sense of smell, and most of us
haven't developed it. Even without paying special attention to it,
however, the average person can

[2] If you're interested in the complexity of smell, read the wonderful
article by Professor Richard Axel, *The Molecular Logic of Smell*, Octo-
ber 1995 *Scientific American Magazine*.

identify over 10,000 odors, and can detect them from a very small source; my wife can spot someone smoking on an airplane 15 rows away, with her eyes closed.

An interest in wine gives us the opportunity to develop our sense of smell, and permits us to enter into a world of different and primitive sensual perception. And alcohol is one of a small number of substances (like hot peppers) that excite certain nerves which contribute to the enjoyment of food, particularly as we age.

5. Finally, it's time to talk about the brain, because that's where all this sensory information is processed. Looking at the wine, smelling it, swirling it around the mouth, and then letting it roll around on the tongue before drinking it gives all of the useful sensors a chance to send clues about the wine to the brain. This enhances our analysis, and, in appropriate cases, our enjoyment of the wine.

Interestingly, there are two separate ways in which the brain influences our analysis of taste. The nasal sensors go directly to that part of the brain which is involved in memory and emotion. This is thought to be why certain smells create sexual desire, and others remind us of events in our childhood. At the other extreme, data from the visual sensors (our eyes) are heavily processed before the data get to the brain. Then the data are processed in non-intuitive, complex ways in various areas of the brain: color is sensed in one area, shape in another, movement in a third, etc. One of the reasons that taste is such a complex subject is that it is created by a combination of data from tongue sensors, mouth sensors, nasal sensors, eyes, subjective experiences, memory, and analytic processes, all of which are processed differently by the brain, and then combined to create the experience of taste.

With this information in mind, it's time to try each of the major grapes.

French and California (West Coast) Red Wines

There are far too many red wine grapes grown in France to be of interest to someone who just wants to enjoy wine with dinner. Just to spell some of them can create a controversy among the French. *Of all these grapes, the most famous red wines are made from just five grapes,* and I will discuss a sixth grape just because I like it, and a lot of French wine is made from it.

The same grapes that are famous in France are the ones most famous in California, Oregon and Washington, so it only makes sense to discuss them together. And then there is California Zinfandel!

Cabernet Sauvignon— Bordeaux and California

Cabernet Sauvignon is the major red wine grape in the world for quality red wine, and it is grown throughout the world. It's a dark, small grape that makes a dark, tannic, strong, long-lasting wine that is said to have a nose and taste reminiscent of black currants and cedarwood. Different climates and soils have a significant effect on the flavor of the grape, so there is no substitute for trying to remember the region from which the wine comes. There is so much Cabernet Sauvignon wine—pure and mixed—on the market that you just must buy a few bottles and try them together in a wine tasting to see the differences, and decide which you prefer. Excellent Cabernet is made in Napa Valley, Chile, and Australia, as well as Bordeaux. Cabernet wines made in cooler regions than those may have a less pleasant flavor.

The most famous wines of France are made in Bordeaux, an area on the west coast of France. The traditional Bordeaux wine is a blend of three or four grapes, Cabernet Sauvignon (approximately 60%), Merlot (approximately 30%) Cabernet Franc (approximately 5-10%), and Petit Verdot (5-10%). The percentages are varied from year to year and from Chateau to Chateau, depending on how well each crop of grapes does, what vines were planted at each Chateau, and depending on the mix of flavors and tannins desired. The blender tries to meld the grape flavor of the Cabernet, the softness of the Merlot, and the structure of the Cabernet Franc. Others say that in many years, Cabernet by itself is just too tannic, too dark, and too dense, and it has to be watered down with juice that is lighter and more floral. Since Merlot and Cabernet Franc meet those requirements, by planting some of each of these vines, the producer can always be sure that one or the other of those vines will be available for blending each year.

Much wine is still blended from these grapes, but there has been a trend, (particularly in California), to produce wines from a single variety of grape. So one presently finds a lot of wine that is made from 100% Cabernet Sauvignon, or 100% Merlot.

By and large, Cabernet Sauvignon benefits from a few years of aging in the bottle. The great Bordeaux wines, of course, improve after many years in the bottle, but typically Bordeaux starts to decline anywhere from five to 10 years after bottling. The price range of Bordeaux wines varies greatly, from $4-$100 or more. The range for California Cabernet wines is a bit more narrow, but can still range from the low priced wines in the six-10 dollar range, to the premium Bordeaux style wines, such as Phelps Insignia and Opus 1 at $50-100 per bottle.

The Merlot Grapes of California and Bordeaux

Traditionally, the Merlot grape is used for blending. It is sort of a fluke that there is one Chateau in Bordeaux, Chateau Petrus, that makes a 100% Merlot wine, and it has become the most expensive red wine in the world! Partly because of this, and partly because the grape is easier to grow, there has been a trend, particularly in California, to produce 100% Merlot wine. It is less tannic than Cabernet, slightly sweeter (less dry), and is ready to drink at an earlier age.

When Merlot vines are allowed to over-produce grapes, the wine comes out tasteless, particularly in northern climates. But Washington state produces some good Merlot, as does California from Napa south to Santa Barbara. The prime site for Merlot is still the Pomerol region of Bordeaux, and the major use of Merlot is still for blending with Cabernet Sauvignon.

Merlot wines age less well, and—with the exception of the few great Bordeaux estates known for this grape—sell in the range of $6-$22 both in France and in California.

The Pinot Noir Grapes of Burgundy and Oregon

The next great grape of France (after Cabernet Sauvignon) is the Pinot Noir grape of the Burgundy region, with the state of Oregon fast on its heels trying to duplicate the taste of the great Burgundy wines. The Pinot Noir grape is the most difficult to grow, and the wines produced from it vary the most in quality and taste. In addition to this, some varieties of the vine (called "clones") produce inferior grapes which are also called Pinot Noir. Another problem is that some of the producers take short-cuts which produce inferior wines. By and large, great wines from the Pinot Noir grape come from a small area in the Burgundy region of France. Because the wine is so highly prized, this region has been broken down into many small vineyards, each of which produces its own wine in its own way.

Pinot Noir and similar varieties are grown in many places in the world. However, the great burgundies, which are among the most sought after and among the most expensive wines in the world, have a complexity and beauty of taste that have never been matched anywhere else. A lot of the grapes grown are used in champagnes, but it is the long-lived, silky tasting red wines that have made this grape famous for over 2,000 years. The characteristic flavor comparisons are black cherry, raspberry, rose petal, earth, herbs, and spices. In lesser Pinot Noir wines the flavor of lighter cherries predominates.

The great Burgundy wines have a special complexity of flavor and mouth sensations that are beyond the power of the written word. I've tasted hints of these in some of the less expensive French Burgundy wines, and some of the better Pinot Noir wines of Oregon and California. A small producer in France once told me that part of the allure for him of the wine was that the nose reminded him of the odors when he makes love. Whether or not that is your reaction, the fact is that it's a special flavor and texture, and to produce it requires a lot of skill and effort. For that reason a really good bottle of burgundy now costs between $50 to $150. Add to that the fact that it's very difficult to tell if a bottle is going to be special or not, especially given the large number of producers, many of which have similarly confusing names, and you can begin to see why this is not a wine we drink very often.

Wines from the Pinot Noir grape do not improve with age as well as those from Cabernet Sauvignon, and only the very great Burgundy wines age well for eight years or more.

The Other Red Grapes of France: Grenache, Gamay and Syrah Grenache

The Grenache grape is one of the "work-horses" of French vineyards, and probably the most famous grape planted in Spain (which produces more wine than any country in the world). A lot of it is planted, and a lot of very different wines are made from it. It is almost always blended with other grapes. A lot of wonderful rosé is made from Grenache. But the most prized red wines from Grenache are the wines of the southern Rhone river valley in France. One of the most famous of these is Chateauneuf du Pape from a small city of that name near Avignon in the south of France.

In the southern Rhone valley wines in general are called "Côtes du Rhone," which just means that the vines are grown on the coasts, or banks, of the Rhone river. Wines of higher quality are given the names of cities or villages. Each village boasts of the particular taste its soil gives to the grapes, and—historically—the mix of grapes varied from village to village. While the wines of this region are primarily made from Grenache, as many as another dozen or so grape varieties are blended with the Grenache, according to tradition and production variations from year to year.

Chateauneuf du Pape (which translates to "the Pope's new castle"—the Pope used to live in Avignon before moving to the Vatican) is one such village. Gigondas and Lirac are other well known villages with excellent wines.

Most Côtes du Rhone wines are medium light garnet in color, with fruity flavors suggesting wines ready to drink when young, and they are not likely to improve after two to three years in the bottle. The better wines, such as Chateauneuf du Pape made from the better producers, are darker in color, age for 6-10 years —or more in special years, and have a special Grenache flavor that is quite unlike Bordeaux or Burgundy, or any other grape or fruit. As I've said before, Bordeaux often reminds me of dark raspberries, and Burgundy often reminds me of cherries; but the taste of Grenache doesn't remind me of anything else. Like a mango, it has its own distinctive flavor, and thus it is easier to identify than many other grapes. Sometimes the nose reminds me of flowers, maybe roses.

One of the best features of southern Rhone wines is their price. Mainly through historical accident the wines of this region never experienced the rush of price increases brought on by heavy export trade. A good Côte du Rhone can still be purchased for six to eight dollars, and some of the best village named production can be found for $12-18. In the best years, even the best of the Chateauneuf du Pape costs between $25-50, significantly less than the great Bordeaux, and half to one-fourth the price of the great Burgundies.

Rhone style wines, typically called "Syrah" or "Grenache," are in vogue among a group of growers in California, (sometimes referred to as the "Rhone Rangers"). Here great strides are allegedly being made to improve the traditional Rhone grape varieties. Results vary.

Gamay

This grape is famous for only one reason: it is the basis of Beaujolais, one of the most popular wines in the world. Almost all the vines planted in the Beaujolais region of France, between Champagne and the Rhone valley, are Gamay.

Like the southern Rhone valley, there is plain Beaujolais, often called Beaujolais Village, which is technically one step up in quality from the bottom, and special

Beaujolais which is given the name of one of the villages in Beaujolais. And so some Beaujolais fans prefer Moulin-a-Vent, some prefer Morgon, and others favor Beaujolais from other villages.

Beaujolais is just the opposite of what we think of in fine wines. No one puts it aside to age. Good Beaujolais is inexpensive, light, fruity, not complex, young, and ready to drink. In fact, it's now in vogue to drink it as soon as possible after it's produced, before it gets any bottle age at all. Beaujolais parties are the rage in Paris, right after the wine is bottled, and the fresh young Beaujolais Nouveau is flown to New York and other cities around the world where eager wine buffs celebrate the Beaujolais harvest with Beaujolais parties. Prices range from $4 to $12.

The Syrah Grape: Hermitage, Crozes-Hermitage, and Cornas Wines

This is the vine brought by the Greeks from Persia to Gaul, where it was planted first near Marseilles, then up the Rhone river, and finally on a hillside near the Town of Tain-Hermitage, just south of Lyon, France, where it has flourished for over 2,300 years. Of course, the French claim it was a native vine, and that the Romans merely showed the locals how to improve it. Whichever is correct, writers at the time of Jesus praised the wines from that famous hill, and were impressed with the length of time wine had already been produced there. Two thousand years ago, the Roman historian Pliny the Elder was so impressed by the wines from this hillside that he went to visit it—not an easy trip in those days, from Naples to Lyon.

Syrah is still planted in the Languedoc, near Marseilles, and is the basis for a number of wines of the Languedoc, where it is usually blended with Grenache and other grapes. It was transported to Australia, where—under the name Shiraz—it has also flourished and is the basis of some excellent, long-lived red wines. A few producers grow the grape in California, where the wine from this grape comes out tasting very differently from the flavor of the wine of the same name in France, because of the difference in climate. The climate of Washington state is more like that of the Ardesch region of France, and there is some hope among wine lovers that the Syrah planted there will produce wines more like those produced in France.

In years when the weather does not result in first quality grapes, some of the French producers use the Syrah grape to make a wonderful rosé. But by and large the Syrah grape is famous for making a long-lived red wine called Hermitage, from just one small hill at the town of Tain-Hermitage. Syrah grapes from nearby areas are used to produce similar wines called Crozes-Hermitage, Cornas, St. Joseph, and a bit further north, Côte-Roti. All of these wines are made exclusively from the Syrah grape, except that Côte-Roti may have a small amount of the Viognier grape added, a white grape with an exceptional nose that adds a floral scent to the Syrah.

The Syrah grape does not have the distinctive flavor of the Grenache grape. The taste is more variable, depending on the soil and the way the wine is made, and the wines can be light and fruity, or dark, tannic, and very month filling. The great Hermitage wines are fairly dark red, with the flavors of sweet licorice, pepper, dark berries, and sometimes an earthy or leathery overtone. The entry is smooth, from aging in wood for several years, and there is a substantial aftertaste. The wines are usually kept by local drinkers for six to eight years before opening. In the better years these wines reach their peak after 13-20 years or more.

Unlike Bordeaux and Burgundy, where hundreds of small producers abound, there are only a few large and a few small producers around Tain-Hermitage. And many of the grape growers sell their grapes to the local cooperative, which is one of the most technically advanced facilities in France and makes excellent wine—some of which, they claim, is then sold to the more famous producers to bottle and sell at much higher prices because these producers are well known.

The best known Syrah wines, from the hills around Tain-Hermitage, sell in retail stores for $25-60. But there are many excellent Syrah wines from the Languedoc region in France, from the Rhone Valley, and from other areas of the world that sell in the six-$15 range.

California Zinfandel

Finally we come to one of the world's great wines and great mysteries. Zinfandel is wine from a grape that has inspired an extensive following, about which many books and articles have been written, and which has been responsible for the financial success of some unlikely vineyards.

First of all, in spite of extensive genetic testing, no one is sure where the vines originated. The best current guess is Southeast Italy, but Hungary and Yugoslavia are also possibilities. However it got to California, that is where it has flourished, and that is where the prime wine from this grape is made.

First, let's dispel some confusion. One of the best selling wines in California is white Zinfandel, which I would describe as a sweet rosé. As with most rosés, white Zinfandel is made from red grapes, but without letting the skins, (which give the red color and certain of the flavors) stay in the liquid very long.

In no way would I call this a great wine, except for the financial success it has bestowed upon a number of vineyards that got on the bandwagon at the outset. Its popularity arises from the California custom of substituting a cool wine drink for a traditional aperitif. As a sweet aperitif, white Zinfandel can hit the spot.

But for purposes of this chapter (on red wines) what I mean by Zinfandel is the red wine produced by a small number of California vineyards. It is produced by some with great seriousness. None has huge production, and much of the best Zinfandel produced is allocated in advance to "friends of the vineyard" who automatically buy one or more cases every year, and to a few specialty wine stores. Much of the Zinfandel that we read about in the wine magazines is not for sale in the marketplace.

Zinfandel is a big, red wine that ages well. The nature of the grape is such that it can produce a wide range of flavors, levels of alcohol, and types of wine. When made by the six to eight serious Zinfandel makers in

California it has a flavor similar to the Cabernet Sauvignon grape, but with a more spicy nose and flavor. It is less tannic than some full bodied red wine, and feels more full, or viscous, on the tongue. It tastes of dark berry, with a bit of a mild black pepper overtone. Only the berry and pepper taste of certain Zinfandels permit even the careful taster to be able to distinguish the taste of the Zinfandel from a Cabernet Sauvignon or a Merlot.

One of the best and most distinguishing features of Zinfandel is its price. For a bottle of quality similar to a $25 Bordeaux you can expect to pay eight-$15. Only a few of the very best and limited vintages sell for more than $15.

One used to see, and occasionally now finds "Late Harvest Zinfandel," a fad from the 1970's in which Zinfandel grapes were allowed to become very ripe before picking, and which resulted in wines of approximately 16 degrees of alcohol. The wines were thick, slightly sweet for a red wine, very unusual and, if aged long enough, were wonderful (to some drinker's tastes). They are rarely seen now.

The Red Grapes
of Italy

As is true in every major wine producing country, there are dozens of grape varieties in Italy. Even by the time of Jesus there were dozens of famous Italian wines, according to Pliny, the Roman historian. One of the most famous Italian grape varieties is now known as Zinfandel, and while not much wine is produced from this grape in Italy, it is the basis of the Zinfandel explosion in California.

The two great grapes of Italy today are the NEBBIOLO and the SANGIOVESE.

Two others that are becoming more and more popular in the United States are the DOLCETTO and the BARBERA.

Life would be easier if Nebbiolo based wines were called "Nebbiolo," and Sangiovese based wines were called "Sangiovese," but, alas, that is not usually the case.

Nebbiolo Grape Based Wines: Barolo and Barbaresco

The Nebbiolo grape is the basis for the greatest wines in Italy. The grape is grown in an area of Northern Italy called the Piedmont, specifically in a part of the Piedmont called the Langhe. The Langhe region of the Piedmont is famous for its hazelnuts, white truffles, good food and good wines. Most of all it's famous for its wines, especially BAROLO.

Unfortunately, far too few people ever have a chance to taste the greatness of the Nebbiolo wines because so few bottles of Nebbiolo are allowed to reach maturity. Barolo in particular usually requires many years in the bottle before it reaches the perfection that has made it great.

The four labels which identify the Nebbiolo wines are BAROLO, BARBARESCO, ROERO, and NEBBIOLO (usually followed by "di" and a location; "di" means "from"). Generally of these four types Barolo or Barbaresco wines are likely to appear on most wine lists in the United States. Because of the fame of the names Barolo and Barbaresco, these wines are more often imported into the United States; but I would expect to see more Nebbiolo labels soon because of the escalating prices of the good Barolo and Barbaresco wines.

While there is a great deal of variety in each category, it is traditionally said that the Barolo wines are the more full bodied, and require the most aging, and that the Barbaresco wines are softer in flavor. Nebbiolo is now grown in California, and is sold as a varietal, (the word for a wine made from a single type of grape) but the flavors of those that I've tasted so far have little in common with the wines of the Piedmont.

Almost anything you say about Barolo has to be qualified. Traditional Barolo starts life a dark garnet red color with a touch of orange around the rim, and usually lightens with age. Some of the old fashioned techniques cause the coloring material to drop out during aging in barrels, resulting in a lighter wine at the beginning of bottle life. Newer techniques create a wine that is slightly darker wine at this point. The nose is traditionally referred to as a mixture of tar and roses, but what this really refers to is the complexity of tastes in the wine. At the beginning there is typically a deep fruit taste, associated with cherries and plums, followed by the smell of flowers. The nose is often compared to violets and rose petals. Then the power of the wine begins to convey a whole new group of flavors with scents akin to chocolate, coffee, burnt toffee, and anise spice. It is this complexity of flavors and ability to improve with age that makes Barolo the greatest wine produced in Italy.

When young, (during the first five to eight years for a Barolo), Barolo is usually full bodied and tannic, with only a hint of the flavors to come. Many wine drinkers do not appreciate the severe tannic flavor in the young wine made in the traditional style.

In 1991 I drank the last bottle of a case of 1971 Barolo that I bought in the early 1980's. It had turned light red, almost the color of rosé wine. When I poured that last 1971 into a glass, it was like stepping into a rose garden! The room filled with the scent of roses. The taste was of flowers and spice, with little astringency, as the tannins had disappeared with age.

Most Barolo for sale in wine stores today is four to seven years old, deep red, full bodied, strongly grape flavored, with a nose of earth and flowers. There is, of course, a range of quality from different shippers and producers, and from certain vineyards that are sometimes mentioned on the label. But government regulations on production keep the quality reasonably even.

Barolo, and Nebbiolo wines in general, are typically drunk with heavy foods such as meats, stews, wild game and rich sauces more often found in cooler climates. In Italy I've seen it used to poach pears, and as a flavoring for risotto. The wine will typically improve if well stored for at least 8-12 years, and for

Barolo made in the past few years, the better quality wines can age well for 15 to 20 years. You can only predict how well a particular bottle will age by tasting other bottles from the same production every few years. The great years for Barolo were 1971, 1978, 1982, 1985, and 1990.

In Italy during 1995 I could still find a good Barolo or Barbaresco for $8-$10, and good Nebbiolo labeled wines for even less. But the better known wines are at least twice that price, and by the time they appear on the shelves in the United States the price is now more often $20-$35. And, of course, on a restaurant list this increases to $35-$75. This is a lot more than a few years ago, because Barolo and Barbaresco are increasing in fame, while production remains limited.

The best way to acquire a taste for these wines is, naturally, to visit the region, which is just south of Turin, Italy. A lot of literature is given to tourists free of charge, and producers are liberal in giving tastes to visitors.

Sangiovese Grapes: Chianti and Brunello Wines

The Sangiovese grape forms the basis for a number of wines of varying quality. It is grown all over Italy, but is best known as the major grape in "Chianti" from a particular area of Tuscany, a region in the middle of Italy. Chianti is one of the best known Italian wines. It is a government regulated blend of a number of grapes (but with latitude in the percentage of various grapes in the mix), in which the Sangiovese grape predominates.

Chianti is well known in the U.S. partly because of the pretty straw covered bottles lining the walls of older Italian restaurants. A lot of Chianti was sold because of these distinctive bottles in the 1950's and 60's. Much of that Chianti, along with a lot of Chianti in general, was not very tasty. Some guarantee of quality can be expected from labels that say "Chianti Classico," which means that it was produced in the original

Chianti area. But the fact is that many wine makers find it difficult to create a Chianti that is pleasing to today's tastes.

There is somewhat greater variation in Chianti than in Barolo or Barbaresco. This is because there is a central, historical region of Chianti proper (now shown on labels as "Chianti Classico") and a surrounding region which is also entitled to use the name "Chianti." And because Chianti is a blend of various grapes, the percentage of different grapes varies from year to year, creating slightly different flavors. The price range of Chianti can also vary widely, sometimes with no apparent reason.

In the past few years, there has been some success in the attempt to create high quality Chianti to compete in the international market for quality wines. This same push by Italian wine makers has led to an unusual situation for Italian wines. Because of the government's requirement that some amount of white grapes be included in the Chianti blend, certain producers decided to break with the mold and produce a higher quality wine that could not legally use the name "Chianti." They began designating their wines "table wine" instead of the government controlled "Chianti" or "D.O.C.," which means "government controlled name."

As a result of all this, while the words "table wine" are used for wines of lesser quality in most other places in the world, in Italy today those words grace some of the best wine production. This has created a proliferation of labels that makes wines from Tuscany as impossible to identify as those from Burgundy!

In spite of the confusion with labels, one wine which has retained its style and reputation for many generations is the famous Brunello di Montalcino. This wine, made from the Sangiovese grape in one small area of Tuscany, is an excellent representative of the best of the wine that can be made from this grape. Grapes of slightly lower quality harvested in the Montalcino region are used to make "Rosso di Montalcino," a good quality wine which is often sold at very reasonable prices. It is slightly less mellow than Brunello, since it is aged a shorter time in wood. Rosso di Montalcino is also sometimes made from the same grapes as the wine-maker's expensive Brunello, when the winemaker runs a bit short of cash and needs to sell some wine without keeping it in wood for the length of time required for Brunello. So some Rosso wines are particularly good buys.

The Sangiovese grape is the hot new item in California at the moment. It is being planted in the hopes of producing a Chianti type wine in California in the next few years. Time will tell.

The flavor and nose of Sangiovese based wines is, to my taste, less complex than in other famous grapes. The wine is medium ruby red in color. The nose is slightly pungent, and more earthy than floral. The Sangiovese grape produces a light-bodied, fruity wine, with a slightly astringent foretaste. It has a crisp, moderately tannic texture, and flavors that remind me of cherries, strawberries, and raspberries mixed together. Sangiovese itself doesn't improve significantly with age and is usually ready to drink when released. But much of the Sangiovese grape is used in blends, like Chianti, which usually age well, six to twelve years being typical to reach the peak of maturity. Brunello ages and mellows well with age, four to six years on average, but without as significant a change in color and complexity in taste as the Nebbiolo grape.

I would expect to pay between five to nine dollars for a Rosso di Montalcino, and between $15-$25 for a Brunello, depending on its year. The prices for Chianti vary from a few dollars a bottle to $30-40 for special vintages from well known producers. At the moment 1988, 1989 and 1990 produced the best vintages of the recent years.

Dolcetto and Barbera Grapes

Dolcetto is a wonderful deep purple wine made from the Dolcetto grape grown primarily in the Piedmont region. It doesn't age well, and has a slightly lower alcohol content than wine from the Nebbiolo or the Sangiovese grapes. I believe that is why it "doesn't travel well." That is to say, I've had wonderful Dolcetto in Italy, but the same bottles in Los Angeles have been disappointing. The best known Dolcetto comes from Alba, and has on the label "Dolcetto D'Alba." The wine is ruby-to-violet in color, and has a very distinctive nose that is like nothing else I know. Since the wine does not age well, a recent year on the label —not over one year old— is better than one older than that.

The best known Barbera wine also comes from Alba, and is labeled "Barbera D'Alba." This is a ruby red wine that darkens slightly as it ages. It starts life very acidic and therefore is sometimes not appreciated when too young. As it ages it loses its acidity and gains in nose and flavor. While it does not age as well as Barolo or Barbaresco, three to six years is generally appropriate. Barbera is a deep, fruity wine reminiscent of raspberries and pomegranate.

Dolcetto and Barbera wines are less well known, and much lower priced than Barolo and Barbaresco. I see these wines selling at wine stores for between six dollars and $12, and in restaurants for roughly twice these amounts, which makes them a good value in today's wine market.

Dry White Wine Grapes

While there are certainly dozens of popular white wine grapes, the market is heavily skewed toward one grape: Chardonnay. Other great white grapes, such as Riesling, Semillon, Sauvignon Blanc and Chenin Blanc are far behind in popularity. The relatively small production of wines made from Roussanne and Marsanne makes these varieties less known. Added to this is the fact that, outside of the U.S., red wine is much more popular than white wine, and by and large more attention is given to its production. Finally, while there are clearly differences in the taste of white grapes, the differences are smaller and more difficult to identify than with red wines.

The result of all this is that less needs to be known about white wines than red wines when ordering them off a restaurant list or buying them in a store. Learning the subtleties of flavor of each grape is less important because the method of production adds much more to the flavor than does the grape. Learning a few names to look for on labels, and some geographical references will be helpful.

The question we hope to answer from looking at labels and price tags on bottles of white wine include: (1) is the wine sweet or dry? (2) is it a tart, acidic wine, or a mellow wine? and (3) is the price reasonable?

Since Semillon and Riesling are the basis for the worlds greatest sweet white wines, let's defer them to the next section on sweet white wines, even though some medium dry white wines are made from these grapes.

That leaves us with the task of learning how to predict the taste of only three white grapes other than the famous Chardonnay: Sauvignon Blanc, Chenin Blanc, and the Rhone wines that usually combine Roussanne and Marsanne (which can be treated together).

Chardonnay

This grape is grown all over the world, and more and more vineyards are being cleared of other vines to make room for more of it, because of the strong commercial demand. It is so popular in California that the word is almost synonymous with "white wine," such that one hears waiters ask "would you prefer a glass of red or a glass of chardonnay?"

Chardonnay is the grape from which Champagne is made, as well as the renowned (and very expensive) white Burgundy wines. Chablis and Pouilly Fuissé are made from it. Each of these famous wines has a slightly different taste. Indeed, that is the major characteristic of this grape: it can be molded into a number of wines with different tastes.

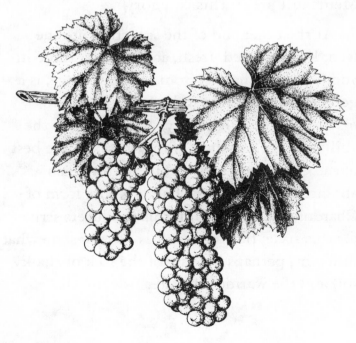

I believe that there are basically three different styles of still white wine made from Chardonnay:

First are the mouth-filling, yellow, viscous, oaky, buttery wines. When you look at them they are honey colored. The nose is of ripe fruit and honey. The flavor is oak and pineapple. This used to be a popular style in California but is now somewhat out of vogue. Some of the best Chardonnays in this style come from Australia. This is not a style popular in France, although some wines from Meursault are in this category.

At the other end of the spectrum are the lean, light colored, fresh, acidic wines more in vogue today. Chablis, from central France, is a good example of this style. It is lightly aromatic, and high in acidity, which gives it the ability to age. A slight "flinty-ness" in the best of the Chablis (from the soil), and with an absence of oak, makes Chablis a pure form of Chardonnay. Many California producers strive for this style; but the result is usually somewhat different, perhaps because of the lack of chalky soil and the warmer climate.

In the middle of the spectrum are wines of mild yellow or straw color, medium acidity, slight fruit nose, and a mild lemon and oak taste. Wines from the Maconnais and Burgundy region are more likely to fall into this category, as are the bulk of those produced on the west coast of the United States. Some of these wines from California have a hint of sweetness not found in the natural grape, which results from the addition of a touch of sugar. (Sugar is also sometimes used in making wine in order to raise alcohol levels).

Some famous names of Chardonnay wines in France are: Pouilly-Fuisse, Montrachet, Macon Blanc, Chablis, Meursault, and Corton-Charlemagne. Of course, in the United States and in Australia (and now sometimes in Italy) the label will contain the word "Chardonnay."

Chardonnay is not generally aged, and is usually drunk soon after bottling. I've found, however, that those aged in oak will improve in flavor after two or three years in the bottle.

There is a wide range of prices for Chardonnay, with prices in California for the well known labels somewhat higher than for the same quality in a French or Australian Chardonnay. At the low end you can find a reasonable Chardonnay for four dollars a bottle, but the bulk of the market is in the eight to $15 range. Some high end producers in California, and well known French Chablis may run as high as $30, and the great Burgundies, such as Montrachet, in good years sell in the $50-$150 range.

Thus, there is no one easily distinguished "Chardonnay taste", and it can only be identified by knowing the label, or perhaps by a process of elimination. In spite of its great financial success, there is the beginning of a tendency today away from Chardonnay in some quarters, toward other white grapes with more distinctive characteristics.

Sauvignon Blanc

(also known as Fumé Blanc)

Wine from this grape, at least in the United States, is on the upswing as an alternative to Chardonnay. The wine is dry, slightly tart and mouth cleansing, with a nose often referred to as that of unripe fruit (as opposed to the more lush nose of the Chardonnay, which is more like ripe fruit). The current popularity of these wines arises from their refreshing, zesty taste that goes well with foods that are not rich or fatty. When not well made, however, the result is a wine with little or no aroma or taste, and sometimes excessive acidity. The well made wines are known for their tart taste and strong aromatic nose.

One of the best known labels is Sancerre, from the Loire Valley in France. Another well known label is Pouilly-Fumé, from the same area. In California, wines from this grape are labeled Sauvignon Blanc, or Fumé Blanc.

These wines do not improve with age. But when added to the juice of other grapes, as is done in various areas of France, the combination sometimes produces wines of longer life.

A lot of cheap Sauvignon is produced that lacks the essential character of the grape. And because the name still lacks the popularity of Chardonnay, a good bottle is still relatively inexpensive—in the range of six to $12.

Medium Dry (Slightly Sweet) Wines

Chenin Blanc

This grape generally produces a less dry wine with at least a definite hint of sweetness. You won't see much of this wine around. Limited amounts are grown in the Loire Valley in France, and much of it is used in blends. In California it is sometimes used to make a sweet, inexpensive wine. One of the most common labels seen in the United States is "Vouvray," a region in France where the Chenin Blanc grape is used to make four kinds of wine: dry, medium, sweet, and sparkling Vouvray (frequently seen in the United States). This grape is particularly important in South African wine production, which is growing in popularity in the United States. The Chenin Blanc grape is now sometimes seen in the United States as Anjou Blanc, a popular production from the Loire Valley in France. Rosé d'Anjou, with a similar taste, used to be very popular in the 1950's and 1960's in the United States, before the craze for dry white wine.

The wine is light straw in color, with a light floral aroma. Its main characteristic is very high acidity, particularly when the wine is young. Because of the high acidity, the wine ages well and improves with age, sometimes up to 20 years. Sometimes this wine, even when produced as a still wine, will have a slight tingle like very small bubbles, which makes it particularly refreshing.

Because of the range of styles, when buying or ordering a wine from the Chenin Blanc grape it is important to look at the label for clues, or to ask, if you are to know if you will be drinking a dry, medium, or sweet wine, and whether or not it is still or sparkling.

The wines from this grape are among the least expensive wines of those discussed in this book, and can be found at prices between three to $10. These wines are now attracting more and more interest, again, as an alternative to the more expensive Chardonnay.

Roussanne & Marsanne

These two grapes, in varying percentages, are responsible for the white wines of the Rhone Valley in France. While still little known, they produce a wine that has, for many people, just the right proportion of dryness to sweetness, a wonderful floral nose, and the ability to age well. As a result of these favorable characteristics these wines are becoming more and more popular, the grapes are being planted in more and more vineyards, and several of the most famous vineyards are putting their names on labels with these wines representing their production of white wine.

There is no outstanding distinguishing feature about the flavor of these grapes, and the taste characteristics vary greatly depending on the mix of grapes and the style of production. The two characteristics this group of wines has are (1) they are not dry, crisp, pale wines; rather they are medium bodied, straw or honey colored with a fairly strong grape taste and medium high acidity;

and (2) there is a particular light and pleasing floral nose that, for some, makes food taste better. The Marsanne gives smooth body and viscosity to the wine, and the Roussanne gives the floral nose and the aging potential.

Some of the famous Chateaux in the Rhone region of France that are producing wines from these grapes, and their labels, are: Hermitage Blanc, Paul Jaboulet Ainé, St. Peray (often sparkling), Chateauneuf-du-Pape Blanc, and Chateau de Beaucastel Blanc. By and large, any wine labeled Cote du Rhone Blanc is likely to be made from these grapes.

Lack of demand has kept prices of these wines down, but the small production has kept them up. Those wines produced by the famous red wine producers are fairly expensive, perhaps $15-$35; but those wines produced by less well known producers have remained in the eight to $15 range, which makes them an excellent buy for wines of such good quality and ability to enhance the pleasure of dining.

Sweet White Wines

This is a wonderful subject about some wondrous wines. But sweet wines are pretty easy to identify after you've tasted them once, and you need very little information to enjoy them. Yes, there is a lot you can learn, for example, about different types of Ports and Sherrys. But that is beyond the scope of this book, which is about basics.

Dry and sweet Ports and Sherrys have a distinctive taste which you can instantly identify just by having a glass at a bar. But there are two specific flavors of sweet wines that you should know about, along with some information about the labels that go with them, because they appear so often on wine lists.

Riesling

This is one of the most famous grapes in the world—(some say that German Riesling is the greatest wine made), with a special taste that—once tasted— you will not forget; but not much of it is consumed in the United States. Like mango and Lycee nuts, it just isn't a taste that has become popular. Because of the shifting market toward dry white wines, some of the traditional production of sweet Riesling in both Germany (the home of the great Rieslings) and California has been shifted toward "dry Riesling," which I would describe as a medium dry, or slightly sweet, wine. But the great Rieslings are those produced for centuries on the steep slopes of the Rhine valley in Germany, and these bottles, (with labels containing long 20-letter German words to identify the characteristics of the wine), are wines that become something special after years of aging in the bottle. This is another vine that Pliny wrote about in the First Century, and some of the current wine makers trace their ancestry back to the 15th century.

These wines have little in common with the medium dry California Rieslings, the more recent (and popular) late harvest California Rieslings, or even the well loved Rieslings of Alsace, a region of France near Germany. Each of these wines also has its following, but they are not the same as the great Rieslings of Germany, produced by this group of old-time, famous producers. There are also a few wines labeled as Riesling, particularly from South American countries, that are not made from Riesling grapes at all.

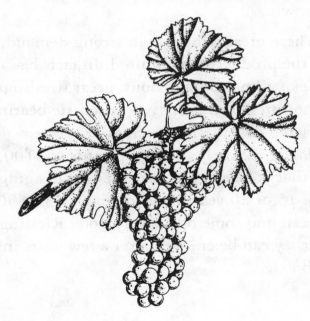

The essential characteristics of the fine wines from this grape are a tart, strongly aromatic wine (like Sauvignon Blanc) with an exceptional impact on the nose, as well as the taste buds, and a long-lasting aftertaste. The taste is as distinct as an exotic fruit, and reminds me of ripe, exotic tropical fruits, marinated in honey. The wine begins life as a green-gold liquid, and darkens slightly with age. The taste remains fresh, with fairly high acidity, while the alcohol level is often very low—sometimes containing half as much as other wines.

These great wines are in strong demand, and the production is limited. In fact, because of climatic conditions, great Rieslings are not produced every year. A bottle bearing a coveted designation, such as *Trockenbeer-enauslesen*, is likely to cost upwards of $100, and that is before you bear the cost of aging it for 15 or 20 years. But for about $30-$50 you can find some of the very good Rieslings, and they can be enjoyed after a few years in the bottle.

Semillon

Finally we come to the other extremely highly prized sweet wine of the western world. These wines are named Sauternes after the area of France where the greatest examples are produced. And like Riesling, while many admire its taste and greatness, few buy it and drink it. The semillon grape, from which Sauternes are made, is used primarily for blending with other grapes, to give them more body and fullness. Not much is grown in California. It is important in Australia and Chile in the production of various blends of white wines.

It is really only in France that this grape is grown in quantities sufficient to constitute a significant percentage of total grape production, and this is true primarily in the Bordeaux and neighboring regions. White Bordeaux, from various Chateaux, usually contains some percentage of this grape. Typical labels of wine from this grape which are seen on U.S. wine lists include: Cotes de Bordeaux, Cotes de Blaye, and Cotes de Bergerac.

These wines are typically medium dry, slightly oily full bodied white wines, which are not noted for any particular taste or nose. They are low in acidity, and thus do not age well, but when aged in oak, as they typically are, they take on a mellow oaky flavor.

But in the Sauternes region, these thin skinned grapes are allowed to develop the famous "noble rot" that, in some years, produces a rich, pale yellow liquid that explodes with sweetness on the tongue, and lingers there for some time. As it ages, it darkens slightly and develops a slight reddish, or red-brown color component. The taste changes from honey and fruit to a more complex, fruit, butterscotch, slightly less sweet, and sometimes slightly burnt flavor unique to this grape. While much of the production is drunk during the first five years after bottling, to achieve this special flavor aging between ten to twenty years is common.

Far and away the most famous producer of this kind of wine is Chateau d'Yquem in the Sauternes area of France. Wines from this Chateau are collected each year (that the wine is produced, which is not every year) by thousands of collectors. As a result, the price of these wines is beyond the point of interest to most wine drinkers. Bottles from the lesser years are now at $100 or more, and from the good years often $200 and up. The small, half-sized bottles are quite popular and can be found in many wine stores, but not in much quantity.

Another Chateau in Sauternes that is well known, but whose wine is much less expensive is Chateau Rieussec; a number of other chateaux in the Sauternes region produce a slightly lesser example of this wine. Adjacent to the Sauternes region is Barsac, with very similar, but slightly less sweet wines.

So when you see Sauternes or Barsac on a wine list, expect it to be very sweet. This does not necessarily mean that it is a dessert wine (although it is frequently listed that way on winelists). Many wine drinkers like a sweet wine with a fruit course, or with some very rich dishes, such as goose liver paté.

Rosé, Sparkling and Other Wines

There are so many grapes and wines that I haven't mentioned. There are the wonderful wines made from the Trebbiano grapes of Italy. Everyone knows something about Champagne. In many areas of Europe sparkling wines, including sparkling red wines (such as Lambrusco in the Veneto region of Northern Italy) are preferred by most of the local wine drinking population. There are hundreds of wonderful local red wines throughout Europe. But they're not on U.S. wine lists very often, and what I've written about is enough to learn for a beginning. Except for the Rosé wines. It's nice to know something about them.

Rosé wine is made from red grapes. The grape skins, which give red wine its color and tannin, are not left in contact with the juice for very long, so the juice doesn't become as red as it otherwise would. This makes the wine rose colored, less tannic, and more delicate in flavor—all depending on the winemaker's decision on how long to leave the skins in contact with the juice. Because of the range of decision that the winemaker has, some consider rosé wine to have a wider range of flavors than red or white wines.

The southern French have a saying that goes: a wine drinker begins by enjoying white wine, matures into preferring red wine, and ends up loving rosé.

There is some truth to that in the south of France. Located in a hot part of a country that loves red wine, chilled rosé is a good substitute during hot weather, and has become very popular. But, by and large, that hasn't become the case in the United States, although in the 1950's sparkling rosé from Portugal became a fad, and the medium sweet Rosé d'Anjou was moderately popular.

Today there is only one rosé that is on virtually every California wine list: white Zinfandel, a medium sweet, full bodied, rich rose colored wine. The huge financial success of this wine is at odds with the trend toward lighter Chardonnay. It may indicate that there are a number of wine drinkers who don't care for light, acidic white wines and would appreciate some of the less dry, full bodied white wines I've mentioned before, if they knew about them and could identify them on a wine list.

Perhaps rosé other than white Zinfandel will make a comeback soon. That would be good news for many wine drinkers because there are interesting rosé wines of almost every character. Those most popular in the South of France, such as Chateau Minuty, are very dry, and hard to distinguish from white wines except for a slightly stronger flavor. The rosé wines of Anjou and the Loire valley tend to be slightly sweet, with a floral nose and flavor. Many of the California rosé wines are fairly sweet.

But in France and Italy rosé is made from many of the leading red grapes. I recently had a delightful rosé in the hills of San Damiano, in northern Italy, made from Pinot Noir grapes. The wine retained some of the characteristic flavor of the Pinot Noir grape, but was more delicate than a red Pinot Noir.

At the moment, rosé (other than white Zinfandel) is not featured on many wine lists, but it is something worth experimenting with. Unless you recognize the label, however, such as one of those mentioned above, it may be difficult, without asking, to predict whether the wine you order will be sweet or dry, and what the taste will be like.

Serving Wine: Customs and Traditions

Wine With Food

While many folks drink a glass of wine for an aperitif, most wine is consumed with food. Some people have relatively fixed ideas about which wines go with which foods, such as white wines with fish, Bordeaux with lamb, and rosé only at a summer picnic; but I'm not one of those people. Still, there are certain basic ideas that most wine drinkers hold about matching wines and foods, and some of these ideas are expressed below. In addition, I love to cook with wine, and I've included a few of my favorite recipes below as examples of how wine can enhance cooking.

Mild (Delicate) Flavors

Certain foods have a delicate taste that can disappear if the taste of the wine is too strong. This is true of some fish, depending on how it is cooked, and many raw foods. With these foods I prefer a dry wine that also has a delicate, mild flavor, often with an elevated acidity level.

For example, with oysters I like a mild, light, flinty, acidic dry white wine. Those Chablis wines, with a dry "chalky" flavor, are particularly good with oysters, and with poached or pan-fried white fish. Scallops and abalone are other examples of delicate tastes. These mild seafood flavors seem to me to go best with mild, acidic white wines. Popular wines for these dishes are the California Sauvignon Blancs, and the Muscadet and Sancerre wines of the Loire valley in France. There is little doubt in my mind that most fish in California, if not the entire United States, is eaten with a glass of Chardonnay, but I personally find many Chardonnays to be too flavorful with oak and rich, buttery fruit taste to go well with these delicate tastes. As they say in French: *chaque'un a son gout.*

Strong Tastes

Not all fish are mild in flavor. Salmon, for example, has a strong, distinctive flavor. Monkfish often has a strong flavor, and some smoked fish have a very strong, lingering flavor. Most marinated herrings have strong flavors of dill, onion, or other marinades. Cioppino, cooked in a tomato, garlic and oregano based broth, is also not delicate in flavor. With salmon and cioppino I prefer rosé wines, or a light red, such as Beaujolais. Many wine lovers prefer a strong flavored white wine, such as a German Riesling, with such dishes.

The inverse is also true: not all meats have a strong flavor. Many consider veal to be a delicate flavor that can be overwhelmed by a strong red wine. For this reason, many prefer a mild white wine or a very light red wine with veal dishes. Of course, this depends in part on how the veal is cooked, and what sauce is served with it.

There are, of course, a lot of diverse strong flavors. Spicy food is one category. Personally, I prefer beer with spicy foods, but a fruity Côte du Rhone, or not-too-dry rosé is also good.

Then of course there are the strong flavors of certain meats; barbecue and wild game are examples. The full bodied red wines are usually preferred for these flavors, such as Barolo, Hermitage, Zinfandel and Côte du Rhones.

Good Bordeaux and Burgundies, of course, can go well with such flavors, but traditionally the top notch wines are usually reserved for foods that will not detract too much from the flavors of the wines; in other words, a really good Bordeaux or Burgundy should be the star flavor of the course, not an assistant. A good Bordeaux, for me, goes particularly well with a plain, simply cooked steak. The explosive taste of a fine Burgundy, for me, calls for light, simple foods that do not interfere with the taste of the wine.

Traditional Pairings

Since food and wine are strongly influenced by culture, there are, naturally, certain food and wine combinations that are often thought of together, whether it makes sense or not.

The French like rich goose liver (foie gras) with sweet Sauternes, particularly in December. I can remember having this combination at a wine bar across from the Church of the Madelaine in Paris, and thinking I was in heaven!

In many fine restaurants, Bordeaux is recommended with lamb dishes. Personally I prefer Burgundy with lamb, and Bordeaux with beef.

In the Piedmont, Barolo is served with wild game and rich, fatty red meats.

Chicken dishes are often served with Beaujolais or a light Burgundy, depending on the sauce. The custom is to serve darker wines with tomato based sauces, light red wines with natural sauces, and fruity white wines with sauces based on white wine or Champagne.

These traditional combinations are worth knowing about, and following, but the trend in cooking during the past decade has been more experimental, and much less rigid. Salmon is often served now in red wine sauce, and white wine with various herbs is frequently used as the base, along with stock, for meat sauces. The recent trend toward drinking red wine, for health reasons, has led toward an attitude of "red wine with anything."

With such combinations now in vogue, most of the traditional rules no longer apply, except the basic rule with which we started the chapter:

> foods that have a delicate taste require delicate wines so that the taste of the food is not obscured; strong flavored foods need full bodied wines that can stand up to the flavor of the food.

On the following pages are a few basic recipes that use wine (in different ways) and are very easy and quick to make.

The Instant Gourmet

Cabbage and Bones in Barolo

Cooking vegetables in wine improves their flavor because the wine is absorbed into the vegetables, as this recipe demonstrates:

Grate a white onion into a large pan with a good cover on top of the stove. I use a pan 14 inches in diameter and about 2 inches high. Sauté the onion in a small amount of olive oil, with or without a few pieces of bacon. Drain out the fat/oil, and add some ribs—pork, lamb, or beef. Adding cut-up chicken or duck is good, but optional. Or you can use a mixture of these meats. If you're using this as a main course with meat, put in enough meat to serve four to six people. Brown the meat to cook off the fat. Meanwhile dice up a whole purple cabbage into small pieces. When the meat is browned, add the cabbage (or as much as your pot will take). Add some seasoning to accompany both the kind of meat you used and your taste. I like lamb or pork ribs and then add sage; with chicken I use tarragon. If you like salt, sprinkle some into the pot. Then pour about a third of a bottle of the Barolo you're drinking with dinner into the pot; it should be enough wine to wet the cabbage, and leave about 1/4 inch in the bottom of the pot. Add a capful of aged balsamic vinegar and a pinch of sugar. Stir the seasonings around, cover the pot loosely, leaving a small opening on one side, and let it cook on a low fire for about an hour, until the wine is fully absorbed into the cabbage, and the cabbage has changed texture and darkened in color. Open another bottle of Barolo as a backup, and serve to four to six people. If you're too cheap to serve Barolo, use Barbera.

Chicken in Champagne Sauce

White wine is often mixed with butter and cream to create a rich sauce:

Brown an onion in butter and a couple of large crushed or chopped garlic cloves in a

wide stove-top pan, and then add pieces of
chicken and brown them until the fat is off
the skin and the skin is brown. Add half a
can of chicken broth (if its not the salt free
kind, it will contain enough salt for this
dish) and an equal amount of a medium dry
(that is, slightly sweet) white wine, or champagne (I find that works best here) depending
on your taste preferences for salty or sweet
foods. Put a cover on loosely, so steam can get
out, and stew the chicken over a low flame
for 30 to 40 minutes until it is cooked
through. Take the chicken out of the pan,
and put it into a covered pot to keep it
warm. Then turn up the fire and reduce the
wine sauce by one-third or so. When it's
reduced, turn the fire down to low, add an
amount of cream approximately equal to one-
half the amount of liquid left after the reduction. Stir the sauce, and put the chicken back
in to warm up. Serve the chicken with rice or
noodles and spoon some sauce over both.

Sautéed Duck Breast Through Rose Colored Glasses

With fowl and game birds red or rosé wine is often combined with a stewed fruit or fruit jam/jelly as an agent to add fruit flavor and thickening. This dish is easier to make if you buy only the breast, either whole or sliced. But, if you're a purist you can buy a fresh or frozen duck (or goose), thaw out the frozen bird overnight, and roast or grill the duck for 30 minutes either on a hot grill, or in the oven at 375 degrees. Then slice several pieces from the breast and thighs. You may prefer to use a cut up duck. The important thing is to get some of the fat out before the sautéing process begins. If you start with a boned breast, cook it through on the grill or in the oven (about 10 minutes) to make it easier to slice, then slice it into thin slices. Sprinkle a pinch of salt over it if you like. Sauté the slices in olive oil 5 minutes or so until cooked through, then take them out

and put on a covered plate. Add a cup of a
dry or medium rosé, such as a Rosé D'anjou
or one of the many roses from the Côte du
Rhone, and boil the hell out of it until it's
reduced by one-half. Then add a spoonful of
seedless raspberry jam (or some other dark
berry), and stir it into the sauce. Keep reduc-
ing the sauce until it begins to thicken, then
put the slices back in to warm them up for a
minute, and serve. I like it over wild rice.

Steak in Red Wine Sauce

This traditional recipe illustrates the use of
wine reduction sauce in a skillet-based dish.

Sauté a sliced onion and a crushed garlic
clove in a quarter stick of butter, with a
pinch of salt. Add a dollop of olive oil to
keep the butter from burning. Brown one
filet per person in the butter and onion, until
almost done to your taste. Take out the steak
and put it on a slice of toast with the crusts
cut off. Some people add a slice of fois gras
on top of the toast. Pour about one-quarter
cup of a full bodied red wine and one-quarter

cup of canned beef boullion into the skillet, turn up the fire, and cook the hell out of it until it is reduced down to about three table-spoon of sauce per filet (this will take some time, and the sauce will thicken quite a bit). Spoon the sauce over the filets, add a mush-room cap or piece of black truffle on top, and serve with a full bodied red wine and a sharp knife to anyone with cholesterol under 200.

Haroset

This middle-eastern dish makes a wonderful appetizer on a hot summer night, and illus-trates a typical use of wine as a fruit marinade. Peel and cut into small bite sized pieces, one apple per serving, pouring lemon juice over the apples before and after cutting, to preserve their color. For each serving add one tablespoon each of raisins, chopped almonds and dates. Soak in a sweet wine (any color you prefer), stir well, drain any excess wine, and serve chilled. (If you have a leftover bottle of wine you prefer to use that is not a sweet wine, you can use it and add sugar).

Drinking, Aging and Storing Wine

Drinking wine involves many things, such as what glass or cup to drink from, how cold the wine should be, whether or not the wine should be poured from the bottle into another container. Some of the answers to these questions depend on the wine, the time, the setting, and who is doing the drinking. A delightful picnic wine might taste good from paper cups—and I've enjoyed some right from the bottle passed around. But most wine is probably purchased to drink with meals; so the following discussions are primarily directed toward drinking with dining.

Stemware

The term "stemware" refers to glassware used for drinking wine or, more specifically, the shape of the glass. There's a lot of esoterica on this subject, and in fancy restaurants they often have different shaped glasses for different wines. Clear glass is always preferable, so you can see the color of the wine. For practical purposes there are only two important pointers: don't drink wine out of small glasses, and don't fill up the glass too full. Let's talk about each of these two points:

As I mentioned above, as much as 80% of the taste of wine is based on smell. In order to get much aroma out of mild smelling substances the molecules to be smelled have to be collected together in some space. It's hard to smell something if you're standing outside in a high wind: the molecules don't collect, and are spread away quickly by the wind. So the ideal conditions for smelling, and therefore tasting, are to have a space where the molecules can collect, and into which you can put your nose so as to draw these molecules into your smell system.

An adequately large glass bowl, filled less than half full with wine, is ideal for that purpose. If the glass is too small or too full, there isn't enough space for the molecules to collect in, nor for you to put your nose into.

For financial reasons, many bars and restaurants serve wine by the glass in small, 4 oz. glasses. They do that because customers complain if they serve a glass less than half full. The customers would rather have 4 oz. of wine in a 4 oz. glass, than 4 oz. of wine in an 8 oz. glass. Then too, to finish the first bottle of wine and sell a second bottle before the end of the meal, the waiter keeps pouring wine into everybody's glasses to "top them off."

It would be hard to break these habits, since finances usually take precedence over esthetics, but you can try. Ask for a larger glass. Ask the waiter or wine steward not to fill the glass more than half full. And of course, at home you can have the right kind of glasses and pour small amounts into them. Save those small glasses for sweet Port or Sherry wines, which, when served after dinner, have enough strong flavor and sweetness on the tongue that they do not require an accumulation of molecules for the nose and tastebuds to react.

Temperature and Breathing

Temperature, of course, has to do with the question whether or not a wine should be chilled when served, and if so how much. "Breathing" deals with the controversial issue of whether wine should be allowed to come into contact with air (oxygen) for some period of time before drinking it.

In the United States, white wine is kept in the refrigerator, then served in an iced bucket, so that it is just above freezing temperature. Red wine is left sitting on a shelf, sometimes above the stove, shaken up a bit while brought to the table and the cork fight ensues, then quickly served at room temperature. We're lucky if we can get the waiter to open it in time for the first course.

But traditionally red and white wine came from the "cave," where it was about 56 degrees Fahrenheit, and the white wine served at once; the red wine, depending on the type, was brought out one or two hours before the

meal, opened, and allowed to sit until mealtime. Even now, when I am buying wines at
farmhouses in France and Italy, and they
invite me to lunch, I note that their red wine
has been poured into a carafe, and been sitting for a while before mealtime.

Here are the conclusions I have drawn
from these experiences.

First of all, wine does taste different when
it is chilled, particularly when over-chilled.
For me, when white wine is really cold I can't
taste much of the wine flavor. The flavors
come out more fully when the wine is
roughly at room temperature. But still I
prefer most white wine slightly chilled, because flavor isn't everything—temperature
itself is one aspect of pleasure in drinking
wine. So when I have wine in a restaurant,
after it is slightly chilled I ask the waiter to
take it out of the ice bucket for a while so
that it stays just slightly chilled, and not too
cold.

Most red wine also tastes better to me
slightly chilled. Beaujolais wines are usually
served chilled. Remember, most wines are

not fine old wines to be aged, but young, regional wines made to be drunk while young. These wines, like Beaujolais, for me go better with food when slightly chilled— about the temperature of a wine cellar, 55-60 degrees Fahrenheit.

But I prefer some rather special red wines to be decanted (the fancy word for pouring the wine out of the bottle into a decanter—a special glass bottle for holding wine) and then aired until they reach room temperature. This is a very controversial subject in the United States (less so in Europe). No scientific study that I've seen confirms that "oxygenating" wine improves its taste. But research on taste is very primitive. To paraphrase what the U.S. Supreme court wrote about pornography: I can't define it, but I know it when I see it. So I can't prove that some wines taste better when oxygenated, but I know it's true for my taste buds.

Which wines benefit from aeration? Again, a tough question to answer. In general, I would say full bodied tannic red wines with some years remaining before they start to lose body; a new Barolo, for example, just bottled. We would expect the wine to continue improving in the bottle for at least six more years, and maybe 10 to 20. This wine will smooth out, and some of the tannins mellow, if decanted and left out for two to three hours until it reaches room temperature, before it is drunk. By the way, just taking out the cork, as some restaurants do, doesn't aerate the wine. It just aerates the small surface area at the top of the bottle. To air out the wine you either have to pour it into another container, or into the glasses.

Whether older wines that have reached their prime should also be decanted and left to air is an even more controversial subject. First of all, what do we mean by "older." Generally speaking, wine is young for 2-3 years after it is bottled. Not all wine holds up this long, but most do. Fine red wines made for long aging can be called "young" after six years or more, because they are not nearly ready to drink. So "old" and "young" are relative terms, depending on the aging potential of the wine.

Certainly there are times when a bottle of well aged wine is opened and poured, and tastes good for a few minutes, then goes somewhat flat. To have aerated that bottle would have killed it before it was tasted. So in general I would avoid decanting or airing an older bottle, unless you know from a previous bottle that it gets better after the second or third glass.

There is another reason that wine is decanted, other than to oxygenate it: as some red wines age, acids and tannins fall out of the liquid solution to the bottom of the bottle. This residue, called sediment, if mixed into the liquid wine makes it visually unpleasant, and the sediment can adversely affect the taste and texture of the wine.

For this reason, in many fine restaurants fine, older red wine is poured from the original bottle into a new glass bottle. The original bottle is usually left on the table, so that you can continue to admire the label if you drink so much that you forget what you are drinking. Sometimes decanting is done very ceremoniously, with special equipment. A candle is placed under the bottle to light up the liquid (to better see the sediment) as was done in the old days in the dark wine cellars, and the wine is slowly poured through a silver funnel until just before the sediment begins to flow.

There are some wines which benefit from decanting, because they have so much sediment in them that it's impossible to keep it from the glass. But by and large decanting for this reason is a sham. The bigger problem is that when the wine steward brings the wine to the table he is shaking it, and moving the sediment around in the bottle. Then when he (or she, although I've never seen a female wine stewardess, but many restaurants have the waiters or waitresses open the bottles) takes the cork out of the bottle he or she again shakes the bottle around. Whatever little sediment there was in the bottle (which easily could have been kept in the bottom of the bottle and controlled by careful pouring) is now mixed throughout the wine. Now decanting won't help anyway.

The fact is that wine bottles, especially the Bordeaux shaped bottle, are designed to keep the sediment in the "shoulder" of the bottle as the wine is poured, and, if the wine is not shaken up and is poured carefully (and not to the last drop) the sediment will stay in the bottle.

There is probably little you can do about these problems in restaurants, but at home you can handle the wine carefully and avoid the need to decant except for young tannic red wines that need it, or that special old bottle that has a lot of sediment in it. For that special bottle, just let it sit still overnight before you decant it.

Aging and Storage

I've mentioned several times that most wine is better when drunk young, in the first one or two years after it is bottled. I've also mentioned how sad it is that so much of the small production that will improve in the bottle is drunk well before it has reached its prime. Now let's talk a bit about when and how you may want to let certain wines age.

There is no question that those who drank up their 1985 premier cru Bordeaux before 1990, or their 1990 Barolo's before 1995, lost a chance to enjoy something special by keeping those wines another 5-10 years or more before drinking them. But these were special years for those wines, and much of what we know about these wines came from drinking them during this period, and seeing that they had these special characteristics that would allow them to continue to improve with age.

For most wines, even the fine ones we expect to age well, it's really hard to tell how long they will continue to improve. And, to most tastes, its better to drink the wine when too young than when too old (although some people, including me, like wines just past their prime). The bottom line is that unless you are extremely knowledgeable about the wine, if you are going to allow it to age in your cellar it is preferable to have several bottles (or a case) and drink a bottle every one or two years, and make notes, to keep track of the progress.

This may not be as painful as its sounds. While there is a lot of hoopla about wonderful aged wines—with much justification—most wine is plenty good well before its prime. The main thing to avoid is drinking really big wines when very young. I remember tasting a late harvest Zinfandel when it was four years old, and it was terrible. Only after about 15 years in the bottle did it become drinkable, and then, at age 20, it was wonderful. I've had similar experiences with Bordeaux and Barolo on a lesser time scale: drinking them one or two years after bottling, and finding them too tannic and without much flavor, then finding great improvement after 4-5 years.

As wine ages, it changes. Take Bordeaux as an example. As really well made Bordeaux ages the color fades from deep red with a purple tint, to a more red brick color, particularly around the edges. When young the taste is of cherries and plums and dark berries, with some herbs, wood and oak. As the wine ages these tastes subside, and evolve into a more complex flavor of spicy berries with scents of tobacco and dried fruits. The tannins lessen, making for a more mellow feel in the mouth, and the aftertaste deepens.

If you want to put aside some wines to age, there are several ways to do it. Wine should be kept with the bottles on their sides so that the corks remain moist, in a dark room where light cannot affect the wine. The two biggest enemies to proper wine storage are movement and change in temperature. The bottles should remain still, at a steady temperature. Change in temperature causes the corks to swell or shrink, and this is why you should examine a bottle served in a restaurant before it is opened, so that you can see if the cork is intact.

Many homes have an area in the back of a closet on the ground floor that is relatively cool, gets no sun or heat, and is adequate to age wines. Wines aged at room temperature, however, will age more quickly than those kept at the ideal temperature of 55 to 60 degrees farenheit, and the slower aging process is preferable. Wine lockers which keep wines at the preferred temperature are for rent at very reasonable rates in many wine stores. Or you can buy any one of a number of different wine storage cabinets made for the home which are cooled electrically. These come in different sizes, styles and qualities. There are also companies which fit a home closet or basement with a cooling unit, to make a professional-like storage area.

Only through reading about the wines, and from personal experience with aged wines, will you come to fully appreciate properly aged wines.

Wine and Health

In the United States there are many people who harbor an innate distrust of alcohol, which is why it is so heavily regulated. Maybe this is because alcohol was heavily abused during the early part of our history. Then too, the fact that we have become a society so dominated by the automobile, and the fact that alcohol does increase the risk of error in driving, has given legitimacy to concerns over the improper use of alcohol.

As a result of this distrust, and these concerns, drinking in general, including moderate servings of wine with dinner, is frowned upon by many people in our society. But, as a result of recent medical research, these attitudes may be changing, and we may be at the beginning of an accelerating upswing in the number of people who drink wine in moderation.

It's pretty clear now that regular, moderate consumption of alcohol is associated with a "very low risk of death from coronary heart disease," and that "people who drink alcohol regularly tend to have higher blood levels of protective h.d.l.'s, or high-density lipoproteins, which carry cholesterol out of the body and presumably help to keep coronary arteries unclogged. Red wine, by far the most popular alcoholic beverage in France, is believed to be the most beneficial since, in addition to the effects of the alcohol on h.d.l., substances in red grapes appear to inhibit the formation of blood clots."

—*New York Times* Health Section,
Dec. 28, 1994 reporting on a study at
U. of Calif., San Diego

This report on the beneficial effects of red wine was confirmed by research at both Harvard University and California State University, Fresno. The essence of these studies suggests that red wine contains the same helpful chemical that is in aspirin, and therefore a glass of wine each day is similar to an aspirin a day, which is now recommended by many physicians.

Another study recently reported in Wine Spectator magazine, is based on a report in the British Medical Journal. According to that report, a 12-year study in Copenhagen indicated a 49 percent reduction in mortality from vascular and cerebrovascular diseases in people who drank three to five glasses of wine per day.

Morten Gronbaek, from the Institute of Preventive Medicine at Copenhagen Municipal Hospital, one of the authors of the study, believes that antioxidants and flavonoids, which some medical authorities believe prevent coronary heart disease, may be present in red wines.

The danger in assuming that wine is good for health has to do with the human tendency to over-consume. What's not yet clear is how many people can drink one or two glasses of wine a day, and not proceed to six or eight or more. It's no good to prevent heart disease if you're going to die from cirrhosis of the liver or a head-on automobile accident.

There are other problems with drinking wine. If you are diabetic, for example, the alcohol, which converts to sugar in the body, may throw off your insulin regulation. People prone to depression may become depressed with moderate consumption of alcohol. And people with a tendency to be overweight may find that the consumption of alcohol adds to their weight problem. Combining alcohol with certain medications can be a serious error, so if you are taking any medication it only makes sense to check with a doctor before taking a drink. In general, however, doctors with whom I've consulted tell me that alcohol is not a problem in combination with antibiotics.

As anyone who has ever read a wine label knows, wine contains sulfites. Some people are allergic to sulfites. My doctor tells me that many foods contain sulfites in much larger quantities than a bottle of wine, and that some government agency should be requiring that label on foods as well. If you find that wine gives you a headache, or makes you sick, it might be the sulfites. Go to a doctor and be sure, because if you are allergic to sulfites you should avoid them in foods as well as wine. Many people who think they are allergic to the sulfites in wine are allergic to something else, and find that they can drink some wines and not others—for example, dry wines, but not sweet wines.

For most people, wine can be an added pleasure in life. As is so often the case, excess is the enemy. It's important to know yourself, and monitor what you are doing.

So Why All This Fuss About Wine?

Pleasure is an important part of life for most of us. There are some pleasures that are immediate, such as eating, drinking, and sex. Some pleasures are immediate in part, but are experienced over a long period of time as they vary in degree, like a warm friendship, or watching a child grow into adulthood. And some pleasures are more cerebral, such as those Proust describes in his novels, as he remembers pleasures from the past.

For those who enjoy wine, the wine becomes a messenger of all these pleasures, and more. There is the immediate pleasure of the taste, and the enhanced pleasure of the accompanying food. There are the pleasures that arise from sharing wine with friends, discussing it, using it as a reason to get together. And the nature of the taste experience, connected as it is to the brain, is ideally suited to act as a reminder of past experiences with wine, past extraordinary meals, special bottles, special events.

There are two additional pleasures connected with wine.

Through our long cultural history wine has taken on a ceremonial aspect. For many it is used in religious ceremonies, used to christen our ships as they slide into the sea for the first time, used to wish our loved ones well as they marry or celebrate other special occasions.

Finally, throughout our long cultural history, almost every tribe has been keenly interested in mind altering drugs, including alcoholic beverages. Trances are still an important part of many religious ceremonies among tribes in many diverse areas of the world. Going into a trance today in the more civilized parts of the world is frowned upon, and might get you committed to an institution. But the search for recreational drugs remains a constant in most societies; and the subtle trance-like effects of alcoholic beverages remain socially acceptable. I believe that wine drinking acts as an outlet for this apparently normal craving men and women share for this type of experience.

There are precious few sources of such a diversity of pleasure available to us at $10 per bottle!

Index

E

entry, 20

F

flavonoid, 139
foie gras, 108
Fumé Blanc, 79

G

Gamay, 44
Gigondas, 42
Grenache, 41

H

Hermitage, 46
Hermitage Blanc, 86

L

Lambrusco, 99
Langhe region, 58
Languedoc, 47, 49
Late Harvest Zinfandel, 53
legs, 25
limbic system, 27
lipoproteins, 137
Lirac, 42
Loire Valley, 79
Lycee nuts, 90

M

Macon Blanc, 77
Marsanne, 73, 85
Marseilles, 46
Merlot, 35
Meursault, 76, 77
Montalcino, 65
Montrachet, 77
Morgon, 45
Moulin-a-Vent, 45
Muscadet, 106

N

Napa Valley, 34
nasal passages, 27
Nebbiolo, 57
noble rot, 94
nose, 19

O

oxygenating, 126

P

palate, 18
Paul Jaboulet Aine, 86
Petit Verdot, 35
Piedmont, 58
Pinot Noir, 38
Pliny the Elder, 46
port, 10, 89